What Can

Cats Do?

What
Can
Cats
Do?

Written and illustrated by
Abner Graboff

Bodleian Children's Books

I've never seen a cat shaving.

I can't lick milk like

they lick milk.

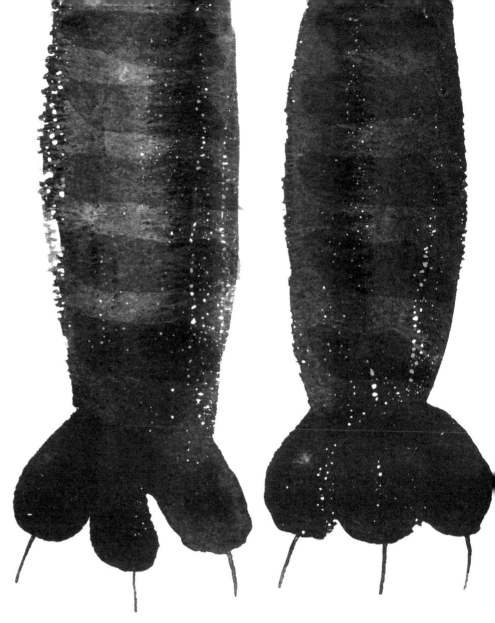

I can't make my
toenails go
in and out ...
I tried.

I've never seen a cat
have new pads put o

ts feet.

I've never seen

a cat paint its stripes.

I don't know
if a cat's fur coat
has a secret
zipper.

I've never seen a cat put its fur coat away in mothballs for the summer.

I've never seen a cat

with

boots on in the rain.

How do cats start their inside motors?

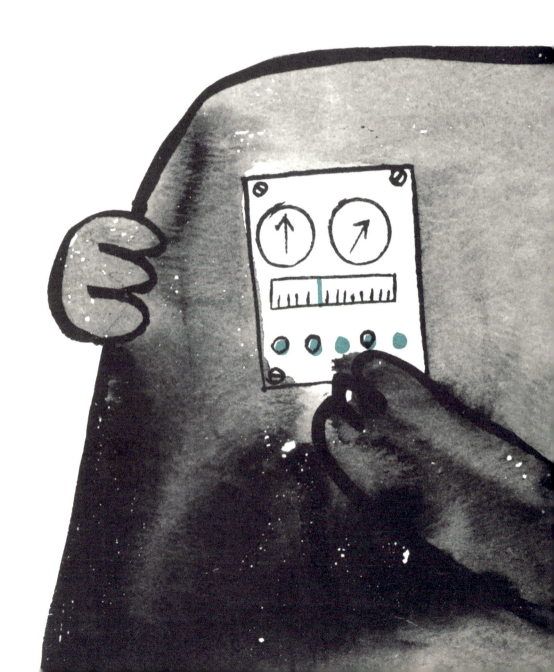

Do cats think their night singing puts children to sleep?

I see cats using
their tongues
as a comb.

I see them crawling
very quietly

o hear birds sing.

Cats are very good climbers-up ...

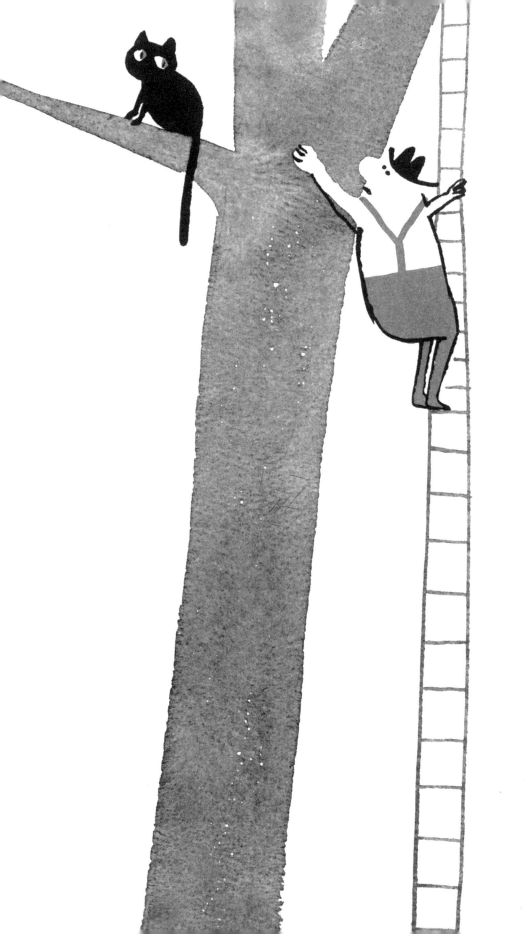

They need help down.

When dogs and cats
play tag,

the dog is always IT.

Cats love

to lean.

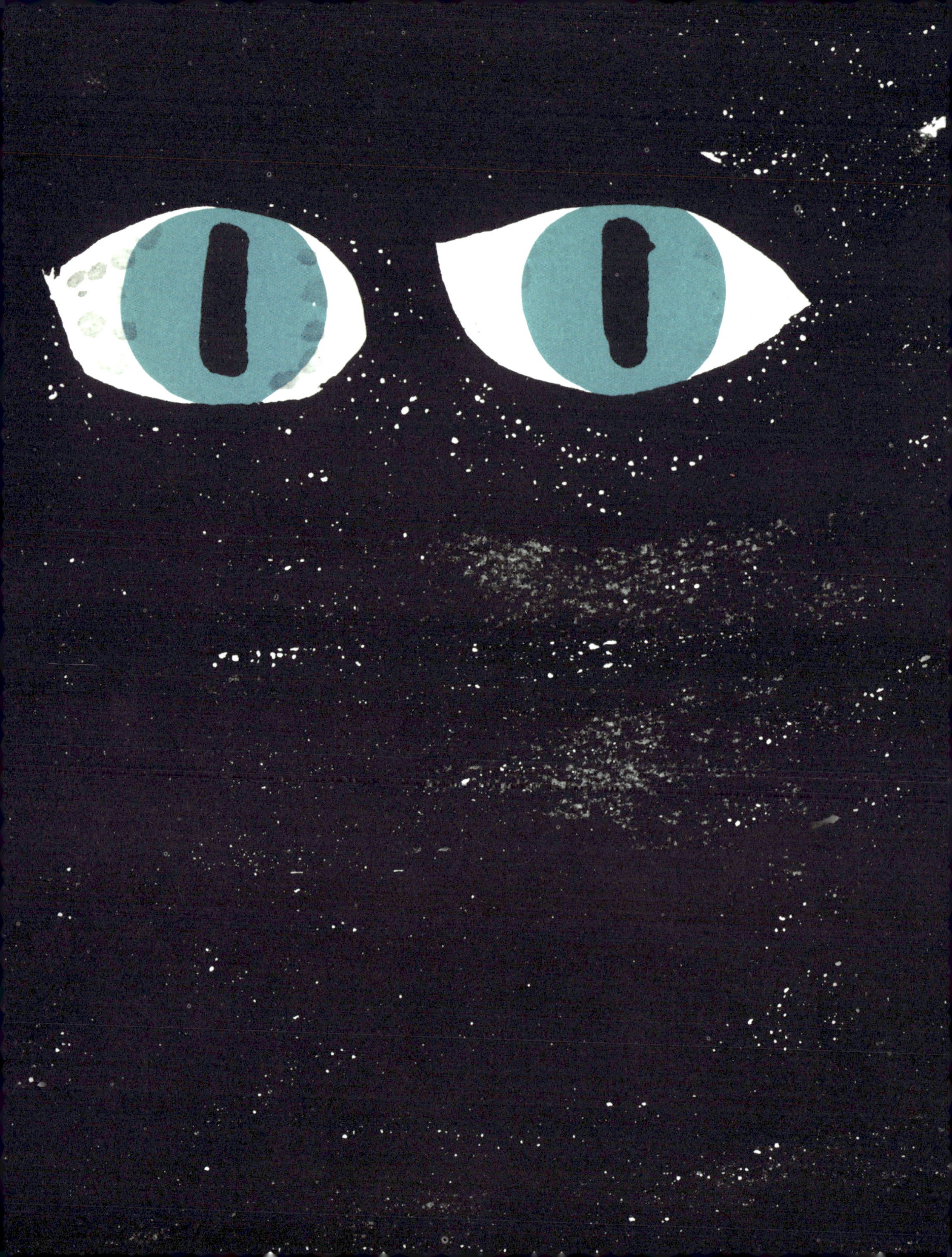

In the dark, cats have lights behind their eyes.

A cat is most ticklish under its chin.

I can do something no cat can!!!
(LAUGH!!!)

The Bodleian Library is home to the Iona and Peter Opie
Collection of Children's Books, one of the largest and most
important collections of children's books in the English language.

Published in 2018 by the Bodleian Library
Broad Street, Oxford OX1 3BG

www.bodleianshop.co.uk

ISBN: 978 1 85124 493 5

Designed and typeset by Dot Little at the
Bodleian Library in 38/45.6pt Monotype Clarendon.
Printed and bound by Toppan, China on
150gsm Senbo Munk Dkal FSC paper.

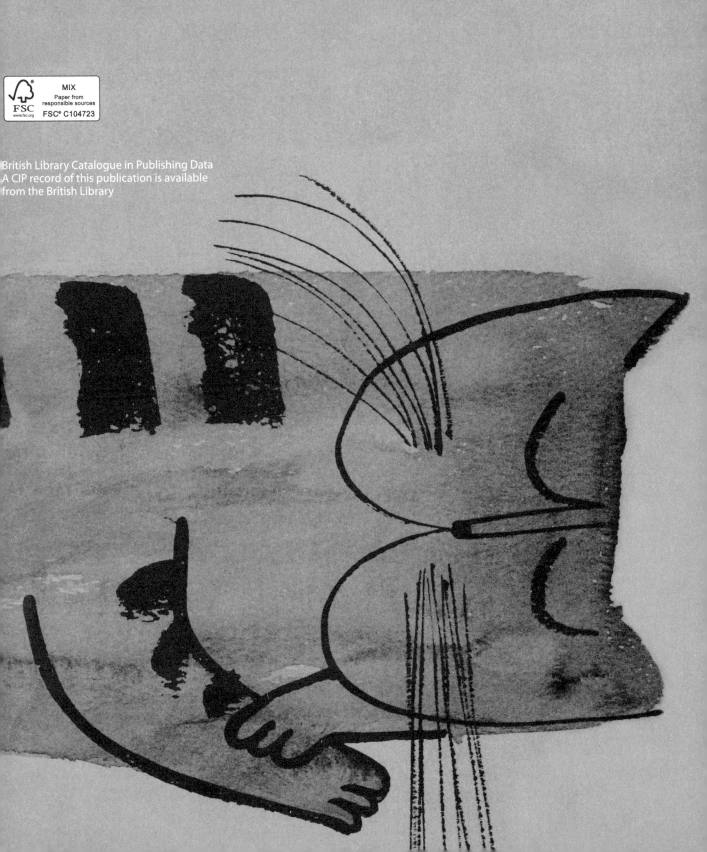

British Library Catalogue in Publishing Data
A CIP record of this publication is available
from the British Library

MIX
Paper from
responsible sources
FSC® C104723
FSC
www.fsc.org